FOGARAS CSONGOR

MY TOP 100 LIFE LESSONS

trust me, I'm an experienced loser

Dear Reader!

I would like to draw your attention to the fact that I translated the book in its entirety into English myself.

Given that I don't speak English, note that the book was written with an accent!

This book is a funny and sometimes cruelly ironic, and overly obscene guide, inspired mostly by my own thoughts. However, much of the advice comes from people who are smarter than me, or even from idiots who made very-very big mistakes and then drew the right conclusions.

I add explanations or short stories to some of the advice, some of which I just describe and allow to stand on its own.

This book is not intended to be a work of fiction, nor to serve as a university subject, but in the reality of everyday life, it stands its ground perfectly with its raw style.

Very important! The book is not a novel, don't read it in one day! I ask You to allow time for advice, to argue with them, to develop Your own thoughts on the topics. This book encourages thinking.

Talk to me through the book so you can get to know my thoughts and -who knows- maybe You learn new information about yourself as well. Get in the habit of trying to take a few minutes every day to ponder these!

Lets get started!

FIRST DOSE

Maybe you've been in a situation that your relationship did not develop in a fairy-tale way. This is when we become acquainted with several different feelings and thoughts. Disappointment, bitterness, lies, deception. In my opinion, it is better to avoid unworthy quarrels, if the situation is unsolvable, we must stand aside. This gave birth to the first advice on the list:

1, Pay for nursing instead of cursing!

*

This is where the following comes from. In my life so far, I have realized that our lies are primarily destroying ourselves. I'm not a talented liar, they usually caught me, so I got bored of lying. Keeping in mind who-what-when I lied to is a huge task. It's very uncomfortable when it turns out and I usually couldn't use it to my advantage, so I quit over time. Since then, my friends and those who like me have dwindled, but at least I'm reconciled to myself.

2, The shortest way is on the straight line.

*

Here is a very helpful advice for those who like to perform drunky weird tasks.

3, If you hit a tractor tire with a rubber mallet, don't be surprised if your head hurts the next day!

*

Many advice today are almost commonplace since anyone on the social media can philosophize and share deep thoughts and quotes with a single click on their timeline, making them immediately feel cultured and educated until their next fucking-vomiting post or spreading political rumors. Nonetheless, there are a few good tips among these that are really important tips, some that provide deep thought and a lot of help on a difficult issue, just like this:

4, If you ask me, you do whatever you want!

*

Stupid, clumsy, under-educated people living in poverty, with a disorder, a physical disability often struggle with a lack of self-confidence. I think their biggest common "disability" is precisely their lack of self-confidence. There are plenty of counter-examples who are not very smart, not educated, were not born into a rich family, or have no hands or feet, yet are able to create happiness. But despite the plethora of positive examples, the majority still do not dare to step into the field of action.
It's all about believing in yourself, even if you know, that you're a loser, otherwise, you'll be a loser for life.

5, Trust yourself, loser!

*

It is not our age that determines what we can love. If you swallow jellybean and chirp after college girls even when you're old, you're eternally young ... or infantile. This word is used by those who no longer flick the sash on the floor to hear it knock. There are those who believe that they should say goodbye to their old-beloved habits because they can no longer afford it, because social pressure dictates that they have to behave mature, whatever that means ... Have you seen Trump, the president of the USA?

6, If you think you're too old to rock'n'roll, then you are.

*

This is one of my specialties. I will not comment on it, I think everyone has been like this before, at least once.

**7, If you do not know who the sucker is
around the table, then it's you.**

*

Not everyone is a good person, we don't have to believe that we can only be successful or happy if we live a life that is pleasing to God. This is bullshit. Hypocritical and quite simply not true. I know evil but very happy people. Even if we believe that the world is pink and good always triumphs over evil, the reality is that sometimes even those who don't deserve it, lead to success. How can this be? Well, because they know the Eighth advice! This is not really an advice, but rather a saying from Semion Judkovich Mogilevich, Uncle Seva, as we call him in Hungary. He is a Russian organized crime boss, described by agencies in the European Union and United States as the "boss of bosses" of most Russian Mafia syndicates in the world. Mogilevich is believed to direct a vast criminal empire and is described by the FBI as "the most dangerous mobster in the world." He has been accused by the FBI of "weapons trafficking, contract murders, extortion, drug trafficking, and prostitution on an international scale. This is very a useful advice for me because I interpret health, is our greatest treasure. If we live in health, we can achieve anything. We can move mountains, we can fail and stand up again and again, no matter what our purpose is, we live and that is the most important thing, to fix anything else there is money.

8, Be healthy, we can buy the rest!

*

You can't buy happiness with money ... The previous point leads here! You can't buy love either. I'll reverse that. Are hungry, sick Africans happy? Let's keep in mind that money or lack of it can play a role in both happiness and unhappiness, but whoever seeks the true source of happiness by counting money is still very far from finding it. Food buoght with money, vaccination paid for with money ... I know, it's a capitalist idea, to cure with money, but I think even if they weren't happy to live their 10th birthday and other 70 due to medicines -bought for money-, it would just put a little smile on their faces. You really can't buy love, but you can fail because of a lack of money. For those who do not see this, here is another beautiful metaphorical quote:

9, No, love is not blind, you are!

*

There was a certain stage in my life when I was making money in an unfair way. There were situations in this era when I had to act quickly and effectively against others who made the mistake of not reading Council 10:

10, Do not confuse kindness with weakness!

*

The human brain is invented in such a way that what you formulate for it, it will strive to make come true. YYour subconscious will be programmed into solutions to notice ideas and emerging opportunities. However, for this to work, you need to articulate it, say what you want to achieve. That way you can get your brain to deal with the problem. In the other sense, if you're shy, no one else can help you, though it might be a great pleasure for them too if they can help you!

11, If you want something, just ask for it!

*

12, You will not seem smarter from answering while looking above your glasses, because you are too lazy to take them off and look straight into my eyes!

*

Gentlemen, I don't understand why this can still be a topic ... a relevant topic?!

13, Pulling on sandals to socks is the same as voluntarily deciding to surgically remove your penis.

*

Gentlemen, if we're already here! If you date on the internet... why do you think your most attractive feature is a curved, veiny wiener? Do you seriously think the ladies will find this so attractive?! A "Hi, this hair color is really good, you're pretty, I like your smile ..." message stands for: "I'm a man."

**14, Introducing yourself with a penis photo is
the pictorial equivalent of "I'm a dick!"**

*

If yesterday sucked, don't worry about it today, because then the grief over the last fucked up day will fuck up your current day and I guarantee that in the evening you will worry that your fucking fucked up day, which became fucked up because your previous fucking fucked up day will fuck up your next day as well!

15, The day is over so you can start with a new tab!

*

This is similar to the previous one, essentially two advices in one. The point is, worrying about something that hasn't even happened is just the most wasteful use of time. If it is sure to happen, then worry when it happens. If it is not certain it will happen, it is a sin to waste time on something like this.

16, Do not die in advance, or do not worry in credit!

*

**17, Do not be afraid to be afraid! To accept that
you are afraid gives you courage!**

*

Nature is interesting. Logical. It is always logical and always simple. I maintain this view even if we do not yet know the answer to everything and we can only comprehend many things with complicated explanations, as this is only true in relation to human knowledge. However, it can be stated that nature always strives for the simplest solution, always logical.
Therefore, before you start solving a big problem, feel free to look at even the simplest most trivial options! Simplicity is relative,

of course. For a mathematician, solving a particular problem in his or her field is also different than for a dumbass, who can barely state his or her own age. The solution remains simple, only we can possibly be too stupid for it.

**18, In general, the simplest things solve
even the most difficult tasks.**

*

19, Dreams remain dreams until you realize them!

*

It is often said that the victims of plane crashes did not die in the air, but when they reach the ground.

**20, You don't fail when you're in trouble,
you fail when you give up!**

*

It has happened to me countless times that I instinctively wanted to act in a situation where there was no emotional charge. So I'm not talking about doing something in anger, sudden happiness, in stressful situation, but in a situation that can be said to be neutral, I decided to do something or not do itat all. When I think about it and do it differently, it doesn't necessarily go wrong, but it's usually true that my first- immediate- instinctive decision would have yielded better results.

21, The first thought is always better.

*

This is inherent in human nature. We like to be smart and be emergency birds. However, this behavior can ruin the lives of others. Therefore, if I am interested in the secret of wealth, I only listen to the advice of rich people. If I want to be mediocre, a worker, I ask one how he did it, but I would never ask a man for life advice before he hangs himself, I would never ask for sex tips from the pope, and I would never want to learn honor from a

politician.
**22, Never accept the advice of a person on the subject
who has not been to where you are going!**

*

Imagine two kids in the playhouse pulling a big plush number at
both ends and arguing that where one sees it's a six, the other sees
nine. They are debating the same thing, their opinions are different and from their own point of view, both are right.
23, Learn to accept other people's truth.

*

I have noticed that the more selfless I give, the more I get. This
is another commonplace, but a true commonplace. The cycle of
life: if I anchor and stop my own little microcirculation in some
area of life, it won't flow inward either. If I do not give love, I am
not lovable. If I don't give the money out of my hand, but squeez-
ing the pennies to me in a stingy way, my income won't ripple like
it could rumble if I took part in the cycle. This is true in all areas.
Give love. You don't have to give it to every fucking bastard! No
no, -god- no! Give love who deserves it, accumulate it with love
and kindness, I guarantee that kindness will flow in your direction even from the tap as well! I don't know why does it work like
this, there are certainly human radiations and nonverbal signs
that message the environment, but the fact is that I used to be a
very aloof person. I wanted to love, but I didn't really show it. As
I selflessly began to give from myself, others opened themselves
in front of me. So donation doesn't always mean tangible goods!
Usually not for those!
24, Donate generously and you will receive as well!

*

I once read a very wise advice, I want you to consider it!
**25, Of course, take lots of photos when you travel
somewhere, but always have your friends in the picture**

**too! In 30 years, you're not going to look at the stupid
Colosseum on the photos, but your old friends!**

*

Learn new words and phrases. Not only because you won't look
like a stupid asshole, but also because the following advice is very
true:

26, Your thoughts are limited by your vocabulary!

*

Respect has always been important to me. I don't respect a lot of
people because they just don't have the skills that are aspects for
me to respect them. At the same time, there are those I respect,
but I do not idolize them. The difference between the two is nu-
anced. It is very easy to slip from excessive reverence into what
we call idolization. In this it is dangerous that:

**27, If you lift someone above yourself,
they will look down on you.**

*

Usually, we do not regret in our lives what we have done, but
what we have not done.

28, Do it!

*

I'm a business-antitalent, but I managed to learn one thing from
my many failed attempts!

29, First make it work, then make it pretty.

*

I think this advice would be worth a Nobel Prize nomination,
for if everyone would accept this, we could live in a much better
world.

30, Masturbate before every important decision!

*

Be conscious, know your limits!
31, If you are not too good at thinking, do not do it too often!

*

Many people are either late in doing something or have already ruined something they want to fix. That is why man invented the promise. It's the credit card for "I will / will not do it". In the end, all that matters is what happens and it's independent of what they've promised. So promise is worthless, as are the "I owe you" notes in the bank. A promise is an attempt to gain time for one who goes the wrong way.
32, Do not believe a promise!

*

To forgive is to no longer care about the person's guilt, or the person himself at all. It can be a liberating feeling because your soul is poisoned by the thought of carrying the anger with you. Because of a shitbag, maintaining such a spiritual dungeon within ourselves is more than any shitbag deserves.
33, Forgiveness liberates.

*

"Sorry bro, but what are doing, that you're doing so well?"
34, Doing my own business, I suggest the same to you!

*

You can never know what kind of war a man is at, for who you're new to. If he seems weird at first, keep an eye out, but don't judge him right away, because you can never be sure if he's really like that, or you just caught him in that very "state". If it turns out he's a real jerk, an asshole, a scumbag etc ... you can send him to hell later, but don't rush! I've had horrible openings-first impressions too and I'm grateful I got another chance to make a correction.
35, Try to judge others positively.

The feeling of a slap goes away, but a mockery, an insult, a humiliation can last forever. It matters who says it, but a praise for your love, looking deep into her eyes, can bring more happiness to both of you than just slapping her butt ... but just in case, don't neglect slapping her ass either!

36, Your words have a huge role to play. Sometimes bigger than your biggest deeds ever!

*

37, Never trust a fart over seventy!

*

This advice could be a bad one as well, but as an entrenched hedonist, I think that it should fit into the "misbehavior" category. I mentioned that I am not exactly over-qualified or successful in business. Despite all this, I have some financial advice:

38, Just because you don't have a lot of money doesn't mean you can't spend the little you have!

*

If you get something special, don't keep -an expensive wine- for years! Turn on the TV, start a movie, hug your partner and open up that drink! A special soap you got for Christmas ... don't give it to someone else! Use it, enjoy it! If you do so, you can enjoy more and more of these gifts! If you never take advantage of it, over time you'll only get socks and scarves from everyone!

39, Do not save, use it now!

*

Okay, this is a personal favorite of mine. I was on a hike with a beautiful girl and by the end of the tour my feet became blistered. It hurt a lot, I could barely go, but for a long time it was the most beautiful day of my life. I had such a good time that the blisters only reminded me of that beautiful day for weeks. Then I realized that:

40, Not everything has to be perfect to be wonderful!

*

This is my personal advice to everyone! We spend a third of our lives in bed, another third in the workplace, to enjoy the third third. It's not complicated, yet few manage to find balance.

**41, Have a comfortable bed, a job you enjoy
doing for a salary you enjoy spending.**

*

Warren Buffett is one of my favorite capitalist-minded idol. His advice is really worth gold, here are two excellent pieces of advice from a billionaire:

**42, "The first rule is to never lose money, and the
second is not to forget the first rule!"**

*

**43, "Opportunities come infrequently, when it rains
gold, put out a bucket not the thimble!"**

*

My other favorite role model is Lemmy Kilmister, frontman of Motörhead. This advice applies to anything, if you want to be a rock star or a good person, if you want to be the best lover in bed ... it's true for everything, give it your all, impress people!

**44, "If you're going to be a fucking rock star go be one.
People don't want to see the guy next door on stage; they
want to see a being from another planet. You want to
see somebody you'd never meet in ordinary life."**

*

A statement of fact: A smile, love, sex, satiety, security, etc ... ergo:

45, The best things in life are not even things!

*

**46, It is better sometimes to remain silent and appear
stupid than to speak up and dispel any doubts.**

*

Have you ever noticed that everyone who advocates birth control is all born?

**47, It is easy to be a wise-guy if you are not
affected by the problem! Do not do it.**

*

**48, Going to church doesn't make you a good-christian,
confession doesn't make things not-happen ... Talking
to whores in a brothel doesn't count as sex either.**

*

If you want to do something that doesn't hurt others, do it! Life is short, if you run into the basketball court to play with friends, if you hang in to a concert with your girlfriend to have a good time, do it! Prank is not a sin that would cause anyone to go to hell, but many times they give birth to the best stories!

49, It's better to ask forgiveness than permission.

*

Working three shifts, for shit pay, lick the boss's ass who just wipes his feet in you, courting a girl for years while she's been wading through five guys ... Once you have to draw the line on how long it's worth investing in things. Where you are not yet lazy, but you are not wasting your time!

**50, If something involves too much work, it is simply
not worth it.**

*

WORST ADVICE

Now that we've reached half, let's take a break! Not to be so monotonous, i've come up with some examples of the worst tips!

The first "worst" piece of advice you can get is:

Stretch until your blanket reaches!
With that, they tell you to be satisfied with as much as you have. Of course, this has an end, too, because dissatisfaction should only last to a certain point, and then we just call it greed, but that blanket thing ... I don't know. Why shouldn't I want to be more, change blankets, add blankets, buy blankets that fit my size? Stretch until your ... I imagine these people crouching under what they basically got as a starter-pack and they think it's a virtue. How could deprivation be a virtue, and even believe it's good for them? It is a stupid thing, not a virtue. It is not greed when one develops and tries to get a bigger blanket. Let's take a closer look: Where does this blanket come from? Inherited it? Is that what you want to give to your son as well? This is cowardice. Fear of failure, nothing more, because that old blanket will be there even if you can't get a bigger one ... at least a smart person would do it that way.

*

Do what you love and the money will follow.
I did it, it didn't.

*

Why is that kid sitting in front of the PC all day? Go out and play in the garden, you're sitting here all day fucking with that freakin' computer, you can't

make a living from playing videogames!

Jacksepticeye: $16 Million in wealth, "only" the 8th richest you-tuber, but indisputably the happiest one! Of course, in addition to that, a complete industry makes a living from videogames, testing, critiques, blogs, developments ... the 80s are over, it must be accepted that this is also a job.

*

It won't work if you don't have common interests!

So much bullshit! You don't love her just because she also listens to the same degenerate music like you do! You're good together because you love being close to each other, you become more thanks to your partner and from whom could you learn the most? Well, from the one who is the most different from you! She, who is just like you in everything cannot show anything new, and it's so boring.

*

Be realistic!

Depending on the situation, of course, it can even be good, but I picked it here because it is usually used by "emergency-birds". Those who are more afraid of your failure than you yourself. Not the expected reward, but the risks are constantly being looked at. By accepting such advice, you will never call "that" girl, you will not enter the contest, you will not stand up to a fool to test yourself. Such advice wants to determine reality from the outset. And how do they know what you are really capable of? And you believe them, you believe it's unrealistic to be able to do it. This is how those who could save the world become losers and in the absence of these bad advice, people who seem unlikely become victors!

Do you know why they succeed? Because no one told them it was impossible!

*

16

Don't be a nagger unless you have a better idea!

Well, that's net bullshit. From the fact that I am not a rocket scientist, I can still point out that the spaceship window was left open at the time of the launch ...

*

Forget about it!

I do not agree. We can forgive and move on, but we must not forget, as it was an experience that became our part, it would be bullshit to forget about it.

*

By walking slowly, you'll get farther!

I also treat this with reservations. Let's be thoughtful-okay, but many times we have to be dynamic and react quickly, pick up the pace, otherwise we'll fall victim to another colloquial saying and "you'll be forgotten like gratuity". In today's world, old ideals may not serve a good purpose. Just because it was said a long time ago may not be eternal.

*

Count to three!

Like the previous one, it's not always bad, but if we don't apply it at the right moment, it can become the worst piece of advice. For example, there may be a situation where we have to take the risk before the hammer is knocked down in the bid, otherwise we might miss the opportunity. It is not possible to apply these tips in every situation because we may miss out on excellent experiences that we will regret for a lifetime. Of course, the other half of the coin is that if we don't accept this advice in a situation of a different nature, it becomes the worst decision of our lives. This is especially true if we're pointing a loaded gun at somebody.

*

Expect the worst and you'll never be disappointed

In essence, it encourages you to give up all positive endeavors and be happy when circumstances accidentally change in a way that may be favorable to you as well. There is nothing useful in this. -Leaving ourselves to chance, letting us drift with the circumstances. Waiting so that we can maybe be happy and everything will turn out well one day.- This is not exactly a perception of success.

*

Be grateful, many doesn't even have that much!
This is also a terrible advice. I met this several times as a child and was always accompanied by ambitious, insatiable, greedy, and other markers. If we measure what we have to the poorest, the hungrier, the most neglected, the most unfortunate, we will not be modest, but foolish. To become the same, or to remain on the same level as the most miserable, hiding in the hypocritical robe of solidarity, is nothing but cowardice. Fear of falling, of not being able to break out with all our might, so instead of hiding behind principles, we voluntarily choose misery and brand anyone who seeks to break out of it as aspiring. The world will not reward the humble, as they are humble to accept. The world gives to whoever asks. If he who asks -because he does not have enough of what he has-, he will receive it. I'm sorry, but this is the order of life. He who does not ask, only quietly blames those who are ambitious, does not become a better person, and he who turns his back on this and accepts the rules of the game does not get worse.

*

Calm down, everything will be fine!
Nothing is ever completely fine. You can enjoy it more than you worry about, but there nothing is absolutely fine. This is not negativity but fact. It's just like that, it doesn't make the world collapse, life doesn't suck, it's just nonsense bullshit. Whoever says this to you after an accident is lying because there will be no world peace, or legal cocaine, your bones will just heal and you

will be able to run again. Thats all. Instead of superficial advice, with some attention, much more personal messages can be conveyed, which we can at least be happy about.

SECOND DOSE

My next statement may seem commonplace, or some sort of an advice written on a floral background shared on social media mostly by grandmothers, but think about it! If a criminal is who breaks the law, don't want to convince me that even more laws will result in fewer criminals!

**51, Do not want a sinless life, want a contented
and happy life, preferably in peace!**

*

52, Be a good person, but don't waste a minute to proving it!

*

Steve Jobs loved to think and come up with ideas while walking. Sure, he wasn't the greatest genius of all time, but it's worth considering, because while walking, your oxygen intake increases and your brain works more actively.

53, To brainstorm, lift your ass and go for a walk!

*

The following is another internet cliché that has made a big impact on me. I came across this at just one point in my life when I needed it. I courted a girl. I really liked her, she was a lovely creature, but something was always ahead of me. I made a cake for the date, I got dressed, sometimes I was already on the way and she constantly canceled the date. Of course, I wasn't angry at her because she never encouraged me, as a matter of fact, she didn't even understand why I was so stubborn.

In the meantime, I started talking again to a girl I had known for a long time. I told her about this, and her reaction was, "if a guy would make cookies for me, he could immediatelly pull the ring

on my finger." That's when I met this advice and suddenly realized how stupid I was. We haven't missed a day with this girl ever
since, we talk every day and it feels really good to wait for each
other's messages and feel that I am important to someone.

**54, Do not want to go where you're not invited,
but hurry where they are waiting for you!**

*

"Did you pack your bags yourself?" … No. Carrot Top packed my
bags. He and Martha Stewart and Florence Henderson came over
to the house last night, fixed me a lovely Lobster Newburg, gave
me a full body massage with sacred oils from India, performed a
four-way around the world, and then they packed my bags.
Next question! "Have your bags been in your possession the
whole time?"
No. Usually, the night before I travel, just as the moon is rising, I
place my suitcases out on the street corner and leave them there
unattended for several hours… just for good luck.
Next question! "Has any unknown person asked you to take
anything onboard?" Hmm… well what exactly is an "unknown
person"? Surely, everyone is known to someone. In fact, just this
morning, Karim and Yusef Ali Bangaba seemed to know each
other quite well. They kept joking about which one of my suitcases was the heaviest. And that's another thing they don't like at
the airport… jokes.

**55, Airport workers don't like your opinion
about 9/11, whatever your opinion is.**

*

**56, Time is your most valuable currency, it's
on you for how much you sell it!**

*

I have gone through different eras in my life. For several eras, I
was haunted by my brilliant ability to find a problem to every

solution. I saw only the obstacle in everything. I became a Problem matryoshka, under the main problem, only additional problems and obstacles lie. I didn't understand how to do it. How will others get over their worries while I couldn't solve one yet.

I had a hard time learning that my problems were exactly the size I wanted to see them, and I realized that what I was focusing on was always growing. If I pay attention to the problem, it will grow, if I do workout, then my muscle will grow, if I pay attention to how many red cars there are on the roads, over time I will notice every damn red car and I will feel that every second car is red, if, on the other hand, I focus on finding solutions and opportunities, guess what will happen?!

**57, It is up to you wheter you see problems
in front of you or opportunities!**

*

We tend to feel sorry for ourselves and explain why we struggle and why we can't change, we refer to everything, politics, health, money, family, jobs, wives, gonorrhea ... The truth is that nearly 8 billion people live on the planet and there have been plenty here so far. It is very likely that your problem has already occurred to many. This can be daunting, but you can just google it and you'll find forums, even about things that are quite sick. Sure! Your problem doesn't makes you special, no matter how much you want it!

There are solutions to most of your problems, the question is, do you accept that no one will feel sorry for you after the problem goes away?!

58, Most of your troubles aren't fucking unique.

*

Parents know the secrets, they are wise and you can safely take their next piece of advice because during their lives they have had time to experience its meaning!

59, Do not jerk the doorhandle, stupid!

*

This advice will help with on the less sunny side of life, but hey, this is a handy book!

60, If a fight is absolutely inevitable, hit first and hit strong!

*

The next piece of advice comes from a 100-year-old doctor who practices even at that old age.

61, I find exercise unnecessary, many people overestimate it, forget about vitamins too, and don't go to the doctor too many times. Be in love, get married, have sex a lot!

*

62, A man does not say caffee latte. Coffee with milk, asshole!

*

63, For non-alcoholic beer and for sex dolls pay only with Monopoly money!

*

The more chances you give someone, the less respect you will have. He knows he can shit in your mouth because you give him another chance, he doesn't have to try to meet your requirements.

64, Everyone has a chance, don't give anyone a second one!

*

This is again a popular online question that I would even tattoo on myself if I were interested in what others think of it. -I would like to ask those who have lived their lives like: "what others will say about it" - that in the end...what they said?

65, Never care about the opinions of others, even if they are handed to you in a fake box of "good intentions"!

*

I'm in a good mood not because I struggle with less worries, but because the worries don't go away because I'm bitter about them. But there are wonderful things in my life besides worries, when I think about them, they put a smile on my face. It doesn't solve my problems either, but at least I face them with a smile.

66, Problems must be solved, not nurture.

*

In connection with the previous one, I was reminded of how many people think about their problems every day because they think it means working on a solution. The truth is that watching it grow or breaking it down into bricks are not the same things. These people have almost remorse if they don't anxious all day, as if they are bound to feel bad in every area of life. If your leg has been cut off, you can do everything else you have done so far that didn't require your leg! If you only think about the part of your body that has been cut off - and the functions that have disappeared with it - then I think you are looking at the situation through very bad glasses!

67, What do you have, what do you win? What was it that you lost ... you decide which side of the coin you look at!

*

In the old days, many people came up to me and bored me with 'who said and what' about me. I didn't understand what I should do with this, and then I asked them:

68, Don't look at who says-what about me, but think about why don't they dare to say that in my eyes.

*

Ohhh, how many laugh at me because I have suffered for years with the realization of my plans! But the truth is:

69, Time passes even if you do nothing!

*

People are impatient. They would rather work as a diligent ant for an employer to get some money at the end of a month than work for years on an idea that would eventually make them a billionaire. I've never been bothered by my partial results, because if someone earns more than I do today, it doesn't mean that next year I won't earn as much as anyone else would with a whole lifetime of work. It's not a competition, of course, but when it comes to material things, I'd rather work on my own pyramid alone than building one with my many companions as someone else's slave. If I can only accomplish half of it, I've already taken it more than the majority. because at least it's my half-plan.

70, Aim high, work on it patiently and not deal with the partial results, but with the fact that if you reach the goal, you take the bank!

*

Many people dream while working in the factory or doing their decent, everyday work. They dream of wealth, of independence, or just of conquering the woman they always see on the bus. Yet they do a daily routine that doesn't take them one step closer to any of their dreams. It should be noted that that journey only takes you to the infinite regular monthly salary and is repeated over and over again. Get off the bus, go there to the woman, be late for work, start building your own business as a second job after work, but don't let your dreams remain dreams because these are your dreams, no one has an interest in making them come true for you. You have to solve it, but it's not enough to look at the path, you have to start moving on it!

71, Courage! If you don't move, you won't get anywhere!

*

72, Even if many say so, it won't be true yet.

*

73, If you have a problem with me, it doesn't bother,

after all, that's why it's called your problem.

*

I once fell in love with a girl who was very busy, I courted her and kept thinking about how I could conquer her. Then I realized that if I respect the other, it doesn't bother me if we don't agree with our opinion. It didn't bother me that kindness was left without reciprocity, because the point was, I care about who I love. Unfortunately unlike me, she was tired of not being able to spend time with me. However, the point is that the feeling of selfless love can also fill you up wonderfully.

74, Being in love with a woman is the second best feeling in the world, however, if a woman is also in love with you, there is no better thing in the world.

*

75, The most beautiful joy is the joy of pity, because there is no envy in it.

*

76, The death of the objection is the solution.

*

Here's one that a colleague said when we were just watching the women walking in front of us on the street. He explained to me that whoever is too picky greatly reduces the number of possible fucks, so he would rather accept a less perfect women if the big whole is acceptable, after all, orgasm is still just an orgasm. When an older woman walked in front of us, he encouraged me to say 'Hi' to her, but I noted another criterion that she was too old for me. He just waved:

77, The sausage will cook in an old pot as well!

*

78, I'd rather be sarcastic, because beating the

shit out of another is still illegal!

*

A lot of people criticize me for always aiming high and then fall-ing back. It occurred to me that those who say 'it's impossible to do it' when I try to fly out, laugh when I fall back among them. They, on the other hand, never, for a minute, spent time trying to fly high, so they don't know that it was worth every slap in the face to shit from high on their heads, if it was only just a second, but I managed to be there.

**79, Only those who have been above the
ground can fall to the floor.**

*

**80, The fools make fun of your failure, but the smart ones
are curious about the lesson you learned from it!**

*

This may seems stupid at first, but it works. There is a way that whatever we do to avoid falling, things just get worse or don't change at all. In such cases, you have to let go of the thing a little bit and deal with something else, and then come back later, with a fresh perspective.

81, When nothing turns right, turn left!

*

Waiting all week for Friday, all year for summer, lifelong for satisfaction ... Waiting for something that maybe you should do yourself. Bring everyday life to the level of Friday, have fun in the snowfall and deal with your goals as well!

82, It's not Monday that sucks. It's your job!

*

I lost a lot of my connections because I was always reminded of my mistakes when I got into something over and over again that

I had fallen into before. I don't need those who hold me back. On the other hand, I welcome the advice of those who help me not to accidentally kill myself.

83, Fall-mistake-failure is just a lesson, not a verdict!

*

84, Once a wise man said nothing.

*

85, I feel sorry for those who consider themselves sober and realistic. Because I'm going to make a fortune because I'm crazy enough to believe it!

*

Remember, the terrorists were promised that if they sacrificed themselves, 72 virgins in the afterlife would be waiting for them! But no one said they would be women!

86, Do not wish evil to anyone, it is not your job, they will solve it for themselves!

*

I love stupid people because sometimes I can mingle in the crowd among them and sometimes I can stand out easily.

87, Don't whine about how many stupid there are in the world, without them, you wouldn't look so fucking perfect!

*

Here is another of my own brainstorming. Not asking for help, not accepting when offered, is not pride! Accept it with humility, thank with gratitude, succeed, and acknowledge that you couldn't done it without help ... well, that's what you can be proud of. To refuse all this and to starve to death is not pride but nonsense.

88, Pride is a nice thought, but it does not hurt to know what it means.

*

**89, If you have a crazy friend like mine, never talk to him
on the phone handsfree when you're in company!**

*

90, Avoid eye contact with everyone while eating bananas!

*

**91, Most of the things you worried about
in your life never happened.**

*

**92, Love, relationship, joy, good humor, smile, happiness ...
are all like fart. If you have to force it, it's probably shit.**

*

Once you experience the worst day when everything goes wrong
and you really feel like it has never been worse than this and you
think it won't be any more, then you have to be very happy and
really appreciated! If you memorize every moment and experience all your emotional depths and survive, your every day that
follows can only be positive because you set absolute zero when
nothing good happened. They don't have to be super good, but if
you only have a thousandth of fun in it, you can already count it as
a success!

**93, Force a little smile on your face and you will
have a better day than your worst.**

*

The world is full of advisors, wise-guys, writers like me, and
books like this that you are holding in your hands. It's very important to always look at the circumstances, because an advice
can be both redeeming and destructive, depending on who says
when and in what situation someone is giving the advice to. A

wise piece of advice do not work in every situation. That's why we call it advice, not a rule!

94, "Women and children first!" - Gentleman on a sinking ship, asshole at the dentist.

*

95, The biggest mistake you can make is not to make mistakes.

*

George Carlin was one of my favorite 'thinking idols':

96, "I have as much authority as the Pope. I just don't have as many people who believe it."

*

97, Help with filtering: Good advice is often uncomfortable, bad is never!

*

The money you work for is printed by machines, probably they print faster than you can work for it. World leaders preach about world peace, but calculate the budget to their campaign, armaments, development and maintenance of the military industry, which, if spent on agriculture, would mean more jobs, more and cheaper, better food, less famine and, consequently, less dissatisfaction, ergo less need for military industry. Of course, this is just my point of view, and only my own brainstorming, argue with it, have your own opinion!

98, Think!

*

Shit happens, it's your job to find the good in them, but at least the humor, even if its source comes from mockery. The point is to always strive to have fun in the end, if the result is misery, you did something very wrong!

99, Smile!

*

The world is basically full of billions of things. With living beings, objects, natural treasures, sights, information. Compared to these, our short little lives just seem like a blink of an eye. It is up to us how we spend this few decades. My opinion is that since we don't have time for everything, I choose very picky what I pack in my backpack so that by the time it fills up, there are no unnecessary things in it. So my last piece of advice is trivial, mundane, boring, worn out, and damn general, but nonetheless, it has the most power and it's the best advice I can give!

100, Love

AFTERWORD

That's it! As surprising as it may be after the title of the book, there are really only 100 good tips in it. How frustrating is that?! We are so used to it that there is always an extra, 100 + 5 tips, etc.

Decade, millennium, ten commandments, we love round-whole numbers because they seem authentic and important. Who would want a book that seems incomplete because it has only 98 good tips in it? In addition to the good advice, I hope you found the bad ones useful as well, this is my extra to you!

I hope everybody has found something useful by which I could contribute either to just a smile or to reflecting on the great things in life.
It is my greatest honor, -if to any small degree- to have been able to make a positive impact on you through the book!
These are the advice, the wisdom gathered throughout my life. I would be very happy if this book could be an encouragement to everyone to share with the world the advices that changed your lives in a positive direction!

Thank You for reading my book!

Fogaras Csongor

www.ingramcontent.com/pod-product-compliance
Lightning Source LLC
Chambersburg PA
CBHW051940150726

47999CB00006B/2307